PROJECT SECOND CHANCE
Contra Co...
1750 ...
Pleasant H...

Mollie's Year

Supp – Beg

Tana Reiff

A PACEMAKER LifeTimes™ BOOK

Fearon Education
a division of
David S. Lake Publishers
Belmont, California

PROJECT SECOND CHANCE
Contra Costa County Library
1750 Oak Park Blvd.
Pleasant Hill, CA 94523-4497

LifeTimes™ Titles

Editorial Director: Robert G. Bander
Managing Designer: Kauthar Hawkins
Cover, text design, and illustrations: Wayne Snyder
and Teresa Snyder

All characters herein are fictional. Any
resemblance to real persons is purely coincidental.

Copyright © 1979 by David S. Lake Publishers, 19 Davis
Drive, Belmont, California 94002. All rights reserved. No
part of this book may be reproduced by any means, trans-
mitted, or translated into a machine language without
written permission from the publisher.

ISBN-0-8224-4316-3
Library of Congress Catalog Card Number:
78-75220
Printed in the United States of America.

1.9 8 7 6 5 4

Contents

CHAPTER 1

"Mrs. Stayman,
I must tell you something,"
said the doctor.
"Your husband
is a very sick man."

"Yes, Doctor,
I know,"
said Mollie Stayman.
"How long
does he have
to live?"

"It's hard to say.
But no more than two weeks,"
said the doctor.

"I see,"
Mollie said.
"Is there anything
I can do for him?"

"Just be with him.
He can still talk,
but not for long,"
said the doctor.
"And take care of yourself,
Mrs. Stayman.
Take good care of yourself."

"Yes," said Mollie.
"I will."

She went over
to John's room.
He lay very still
in bed.
The only sound
in the room
was from the little box.
It was keeping track
of John's heartbeat.

"John," Mollie called softly.
"John, it's me—Mollie."

John opened his eyes.
"Hi, dear," he said.

Mollie asked,
"How are you today?"
She could think of
nothing else to say.

"OK," said John.
"Did you go to the bank?"

"Yes, dear,"
said Mollie.
"I went to the bank.
I talked
to the people there.
They helped a lot."

"Good," said John.
"Did you take care
of the papers?"
He started to fall
back to sleep.

"Yes, dear,"
said Mollie.
She kissed him
and then
left the room.

Thinking It Over

1. Have you ever known
a dying person?

2. What could you do
to help someone
as sick as John?

CHAPTER 2

"I don't know
what I'll do
when John is gone,"
said Mollie.
She was talking
to her friend Rita.

"You will be OK,"
said Rita.

"But I've always had John.
I don't know
how to do anything
but keep house.
I can't even drive a car.
And I don't have kids."

"You have friends,"
said Rita.
"You have me and Art.
We can help you.

That's what
friends are for,"
said Rita.

"I don't know
what I would do
without you,"
said Mollie.
"And there's so much to do,"
she said.
"I never knew anything
about money
or the house.
I never worked
after I was married.
Oh, why
is John dying?
Sixty is not so old."

"I'm not the first one
to say this, Mollie,"
said Rita.
"It's just
part of life.
But, Mollie,
your life is not over.

You have a lot
of good years left."

"I know you're right,"
said Mollie.
"It's just that
I don't feel
like doing much.
I'm too upset."

"But you can think
about things now,"
said Rita.
"You can think
of things to do."

"I guess so,"
said Mollie.
"Oh, Rita,
I'm going to miss him."

Just then,
the telephone rang.
It was the doctor.
"Come down right away, Mollie.
We need you here."

Mollie hung up the phone
and looked at Rita.
They both knew
the end was near
for John.

Thinking It Over

1. How much should
    married persons lean
    on their husbands and wives?

2. Do you think
    there are good years left
    after 60?
    Why or why not?

3. How is death
    a part of life?

CHAPTER 3

Rita and Art
took Mollie
to the hospital.
Mollie ran
to see her husband
for the last time.
She stayed with him
for three long hours.
Then John died.

The doctor told Mollie
to go home
and get some sleep.
She went home,
but she couldn't sleep.
There was too much
on her mind.
She was thinking
about the days
when she first knew
John Stayman.

She had been working
in an office.
John came to work there, too.
They started going out.
Soon John asked her
to marry him.
She was so happy
in those days.
She quit her job
and took care
of the house.
She did all the housework,
and John worked
in the office.
On Saturday nights
they would go out for dinner.
She was sad
when they found
that they couldn't
have a baby.
But after a few years,
she didn't mind so much.
It was a good life.

Now all she wanted
was to have John back.

"But John's not coming back.
He's gone.
He's dead,"
she had to keep
telling herself.

She looked around
at the house.
It was a nice little house.
It was
in the city.
But it seemed like
it was out
in the country.
That was because
there were so many trees
around the house.
She and John had planted them.
She could hear John
talking to her.
She could see him
reading in his chair.

But he was gone now.
He was gone,
and he was not coming back.

Thinking It Over

1. Do you think
    it was a good idea
    for Mollie
    to keep telling herself
    that John was gone?
    Why or why not?

2. Have you ever thought
    you saw something
    no one else could see?
    Why does this happen
    sometimes?

CHAPTER 4

Mollie sat
around the house
a lot.
Day after day,
she sat
in front of the TV.
She felt very sad.
She missed John.
She knew
it was time
to start a new life.
But how?

Mollie was getting
some money
because John
had died.
She wanted
to keep the house.
But to do that,
she would need more money.

She thought she might
have to get a job.
Yes, she must
get a job soon.
But it had been
such a long time
since she had worked.
What could she do now?
Things had changed a lot
since she had
worked in an office.

She looked
in the newspaper.
All the jobs
seemed so hard.
How could she do
any of them?
Who would want
a woman her age?

She called Rita.

"Rita, I'm going
to get a job,"
said Mollie.

Rita asked,
"What kind of job?"

"Well, I don't know.
I don't think
I can do anything,"
Mollie said.
"What do you think
I might be good at?"

"You're good with people,"
said Rita.
"You're always nice
to talk to.
And people like you.
Why don't you
get a job
working with people?"

"Maybe I could,"
said Mollie.
"How do I go about it?
I've looked
in the newspaper.
I can't do
any of those jobs."

"I'm sure you could,"
said Rita.
"Why don't you
go down to the Job Service?
Maybe they could help."

"This is all
so new to me,"
said Mollie.
"But OK.
I'll go to the Job Service."

Thinking It Over

1.   How does a woman like
     Mollie get money
     when her husband dies?

2.   What kind of job
     do you think Mollie
     would be good at?

3.   If you were Mollie,
     how would you go about
     finding a job?

CHAPTER 5

The Job Service
was run by the state.
It was three miles away,
so Mollie took a bus.

The woman
at the desk asked,
"What's your name?"

"Mollie Stayman,"
said Mollie.

"Please fill out this card,"
said the woman.
"Then sit over there
until we call you."

Mollie did as she was told.
She looked around the room.
I don't like this place,
she thought.

But she waited—
almost an hour.

Then the woman shouted,
"Mrs. Stayman!
You will talk
with Mrs. Burns.
The desk in the back!"

"Thank you,"
said Mollie.

Mrs. Burns smiled
when she saw Mollie.
Mollie could see
that they would get along fine.
Mrs. Burns asked,
"What kind of job
are you looking for?"

"I'm not sure,"
said Mollie.
"I think I want
to work with people.
But I don't know
how to do anything.

I haven't worked   .
for almost 35 years."

Mrs. Burns said,
"Can you count money?
Can you make change?"

"Why, yes,"
said Mollie.

"How about a job
as a clerk
in a bakery?
Do you want to try for
a job at May's Bakery?
I can send you there
right now,"
Mrs. Burns said.

"OK," said Mollie.
But she wasn't sure
it was such
a good idea.

There was no bus
going to May's.

Mollie walked
all the way.

The people at May's
liked Mollie.
They said
she could start
the next day.

So the next day
Mollie went to work
at the bakery.
She put on
the white coat
they gave her.
She sold pies and cakes,
cookies and rolls.
She put the food
in little white bags.
She took money.
Her hands and arms and eyes
were busy all day.

It was dark
when Mollie walked home.
She was very tired.

So this is what
working with people is like,
she thought to herself.

A week later
she went to see
Mrs. Burns again.

"I don't think
I have
the right job for me,"
said Mollie.

So Mrs. Burns gave Mollie
a test.
The test said
Mollie might like
working with sick people.

"You seem
pretty smart,"
said Mrs. Burns.
"How would you like
to go to school?
You could be trained
as a nurse's aide."

"Sounds great,"
said Mollie.
"When can I start?"

Thinking It Over

1. Which kind of job
   would you like most:
   working around people,
   working with people,
   or working by yourself?
   Why?

2. Have you ever gone
   to the Job Service
   (state employment office)?
   What was it like?

3. How is a state-owned
   employment office different
   from one owned
   by business people?

CHAPTER 6

It made Mollie happy
to think about
going to school.
She could learn
a new job.
Then she could work
as a nurse's aide.

She trained
for six weeks.
The first three weeks
she spent in school.
Then she had
on-the-job training
in a real home
for old people.

She loved it.
It was new to her,
but she learned fast.
The teachers told her

she was doing
very good work.
She was the oldest one
in the class,
but it didn't matter.

At the end of six weeks,
the school helped her
find a job
in an old people's home.

She didn't have to walk
to the home.
She could take a bus.
But sometimes the bus was late.
This made Mollie
late for work.
The people at the home
knew why she was late.
But they didn't really like it.

So Mollie learned
to drive a car.
She had kept the car
John had driven.
She got her driver's license.

Then she drove
the car
to work.

Sometimes
Mollie drove Rita
to the store with her.
They had a good time
going out in the car.

One day Mollie asked,
"Rita, you know what?"

"No, what?"

Mollie said,
"I feel like a kid!"
It made her so happy
to feel that way.

Thinking It Over

1. Would you be willing
    to go to school
    to learn a job?
    Why or why not?

2. Some people say,
    "You can't teach an old dog
    new tricks."
    Other people say,
    "You're never too old
    to learn."
    How do you feel?

3. Does everyone need a car?
    Why or why not?

4. What things do you do
    that make you feel
    like a kid?

CHAPTER 7

With her job
and John's money,
Mollie had enough to live on.
It wasn't a lot.
But it was enough.
And it felt so good
to have money
she had made herself.

Besides the money,
Mollie liked her job.
She got along
with all the old people.
They loved to hear Mollie
tell them stories.
They knew
that when Mollie brought lunch,
she also brought a smile.

She was really
doing something

on this job.
She was helping people.
It gave Mollie
a warm feeling
to know that.

Every time
someone had a birthday
at the old people's home,
there was a party.
Mollie made cakes
for the parties.
She took flowers.
It was fun
to help other people have fun.
Mollie had a good time herself.

One day
Mollie heard
some of the people
she worked with
talking about
going on a day trip.

They asked Mollie,
"Are you coming along?"

"I don't know
where you're going,"
said Mollie.

"We're going
to New York City!
We're going
on a bus trip.
Can you go?"

"To New York?
That's far away,"
said Mollie.
"I've never been
that far.
When is the trip?"

"It's in three weeks,"
said the workers.
"It won't cost much money.
Come on, Mollie!"

Mollie had never gone
on a trip without John.
She didn't even know
if she could do it.

But the people
she worked with
would be there.
It might be fun.

"OK," said Mollie.
"Put my name down."

Thinking It Over

1. What can you do to
   help other people?

2. What would you need
   to take along
   on a one-day trip?

3. Where is
   a good place to go
   for a one-day trip?

CHAPTER 8

The day in New York
was great!
There were 40 people
on the trip.
They saw all the sights.

Mollie couldn't believe
how tall the buildings were.
She had to look way up
to see the sky.
When she wasn't looking up,
she was looking
at all the people.
Mollie had seen New York
on TV.
But the real thing
was more exciting.

At the end of the day,
Mollie was tired.
What a busy day!

She had done
a lot of walking
and had seen
a lot of new things.

Mollie got home at midnight.
The house was so quiet.
There was no one
to talk to
about her day.

She went to bed.
She was so tired.
But she couldn't sleep.

The next day
she did not know
what to do
with herself.
She cleaned the house,
but it still
didn't look right
to her.

She called Rita.
"Rita, come over here, please."

Rita came right over.

"Rita," Mollie said,
"What's wrong
with this house?"

"Not a thing,"
said Rita.

"Maybe it's the walls.
Maybe they need new paint,"
said Mollie.
She walked around the room.
Then she smiled.
"What do you think
of bright green?
Well, maybe light blue."

Thinking It Over

1. How do you feel
   when you visit a new place?

2. How does an empty house
   make you feel?

3. If you could change one thing
   about your house,
   what would it be?

CHAPTER 9

If something
needed to be done
to the house,
John had done it.
He had always said that
some things were man's work
and some things
were woman's work.
Fixing up the house
was man's work.

But John was not there.

"The house is mine,"
said Mollie.
"Right?"

"Of course,"
said Rita.
"Do what you want.
I'll help you."

So Mollie went out
and got paint.
Light blue paint.
She found
John's old paintbrushes.
She cleaned them up.
Then she and Rita
put everything
from the living room
into the other rooms.

Mollie and Rita
worked all day.
It was fun.
They saw the old brown walls
turn to light blue.
Soon the old walls
looked clean and new.

They worked
the next day, too.
They painted
all the little places.
Then they cleaned up and put
the chairs and tables
back in the living room.

Rita said,
"It looks beautiful!"

"It does.
It really does,"
said Mollie.
"But now
those two chairs
look old."

"They're not that bad,"
said Rita.

"Yes, they are,"
said Mollie.
"I must get
two new chairs.
I can sell
the old ones."

Thinking It Over

1. Do you think some things
   are a "man's work"?
   Why or why not?

2. Think again
   about how you would change
   your house.
   What steps
   would you need to take?
   Who could help you?
   How much would it cost?

CHAPTER 10

Mollie got
her two new chairs.
They were blue and brown
to go with the walls.

Then she wanted
to do something
with the backyard.
She thought she could make
a little patio.
She could sit out there
and drink tea
and read the newspaper.

But this time
she knew
she couldn't do it herself.
Not even
Rita or Art
could help.
They didn't know

how to lay bricks
for a patio.

So Mollie looked
in the telephone book.
She called some people
to look at her yard.

The first man
to come
was named Ray.
He was about Mollie's age.
He looked
at Mollie's backyard.

"Well," said Ray.
"We can put bricks
all around here.
Then we can put bricks
here for a floor.
It will look nice.
And it won't cost you
too much money."

He told Mollie
how much it would cost.

"I could start
in about two weeks,"
said Ray.

"I'll let you know,"
said Mollie.
She wanted the other people
to give her prices, too.

Thinking It Over

1. Why should you get
    more than one price
    for a job?

2. What does it mean
    to "shop around"?

CHAPTER 11

Ray gave Mollie
the best price.
So he and his workers
started two weeks later.

Mollie was working nights
while her patio
was being built.
So she was there
when the workers were.
She made them cold drinks.
She gave them cookies.

"Thanks a lot, Mrs. Stayman,"
said Ray.

"Please call me Mollie."

"OK,"
said Ray.
"Thanks a lot, Mollie.

It's real nice of you.
I sure get dry sometimes."

"I know,"
said Mollie.
"You're working hard."

"Oh, it's not so bad,"
said Ray.
"It's a good job.
It makes me happy
when things look nice."

Mollie asked,
"Do you mind
if I talk to you?
I mean,
maybe you like to work
without talking."

"No, no,"
said Ray.
"Talk if you want.
I get tired
of hearing these guys
all the time."

The guys laughed.
They knew it was a joke.

So every day
after work,
Mollie came out
to talk to Ray.
Mollie got home from work
at 7:30.
The men started work
at 8:00.
Mollie and Ray
got to be friends.
Ray's wife had died
not long ago.
So Ray could understand
some of Mollie's problems.

A few days after
Ray and the men had started,
Mollie drove home
from work.
She saw people
in her backyard.
That's funny,
she thought.

It's not time yet
for the men
to be here.
Something is wrong.

"Mollie! Mollie!"
Rita was
running to meet her.
"Mollie, there's a fire
in your house!"

Mollie ran
toward the house.
A little fire was burning
in the kitchen.
The people in the yard
couldn't get
into the house.

"We were just ready
to break down the door,"
said Rita.

Smoke was
coming out of a window.
Mollie ran

to the door
and looked inside.

Rita screamed,
"Don't go in there!"

"I'm going to
use the telephone
to call
the fire department,"
said Mollie.

Thinking It Over

1. Think of all the jobs
    you have had.
    What did you like
    about each one?
    What didn't you like?
    What kind of job
    did you like best?

2. If you were Mollie,
    would you go into the house?
    Why or why not?

CHAPTER 12

Mollie said,
"Don't try to stop me!"

The telephone
was just inside
the kitchen door.
Mollie reached in
and pulled the phone outside.
She called
the fire department.

A fire truck got there
in a few minutes.
The long hose
sent water flying
through the kitchen.

"It's not too bad,
Mrs. Stayman,"
said the fire fighters.
"You called in time.

Just a lot of water.
But you'll need
a new stove."

"I'll look
at the bright side,"
said Mollie.
"The place got
a good wash!"

Rita asked,
"How can you
be so cool?"

"I don't know,"
said Mollie.
"But I must have left
the heat on
under my teapot.
I started the fire.
So I just had to
put it out."

Just then
Ray and the men
came to work.

Ray asked,
"What's going on here?"

"Mollie just saved her house
from a fire,"
said Rita.

"Good for you,"
said Ray.

Mollie smiled.
"I'm glad
no one was hurt,"
she said.

While the men got to work
on the patio,
Mollie began the job
of cleaning up
her kitchen.
It was a mess.
Everything had to be cleaned.

At the end of the week,
the patio was done.
It looked beautiful.

The kitchen
was in good shape, too.
Ray's workers
went home.
Ray stayed
to pack his car.
He saw Rita next door.
"Hey, Rita,"
called Ray.
"May I see you
for a minute?"
He walked over
to Rita's yard.

Thinking It Over

1.   What would you do
     if there was a fire
     in your home?

2.   Are you able
     to look at the bright side
     of things?
     Why or why not?

CHAPTER 13

Soon Ray came back
from Rita's yard.
Mollie came out
to say good-bye to him.

"Mollie, I want
to ask you something,"
said Ray.
"Tell me
if I'm out of place.
Would you like to go
out to dinner
with me?"

Mollie didn't know
what to say.
She thought of John
right away.
She had not been out
with a man
since John had died.

She had not been out
with anyone but John
since she was 21.
She didn't know
what to say to Ray.

"What do you say, Mollie?
We might have
a real nice time,"
Ray said.

Mollie still didn't know
what to say.

"Oh, it's OK,"
said Ray.
"Sorry I said anything."
He started
to get into his car.

"Ray," said Mollie.
"Please wait.
It's just that
I haven't been out
with a man
since my husband died.

But I guess it would be
all right.
Yes, I'd like to go
to dinner with you."

Ray said, "OK!
How about Friday night?"

"See you then,"
said Mollie.

She smiled
as Ray drove away.

Thinking It Over

1. After a husband or wife dies,
    how long do you think
    one should wait
    before going out
    with someone new?

2. Was Ray right or wrong
    to ask Mollie out?

CHAPTER 14

Mollie ran over
to Rita's house.
"Rita!
Ray just asked
me to go
out to dinner
with him!"

"I know,"
said Rita.

Mollie asked,
"How do you know?"

"He came over
to ask me
if I thought
it was OK.
I said
I thought so.
I hope you don't mind.

But you had to say
yes or no.
I couldn't say it
for you."

   "I said yes,"
said Mollie.
"But I feel funny
about it.
Because of John."

   "Really, Mollie,"
said Rita.
"You didn't say
you would marry this guy.
You just said
you would go out with him.
There's nothing wrong
with that."

   This last year
had been a big one for Mollie.
Her husband had been sick.
He had died.
Then she was all by herself.
She had gone to school.

She had found a job.
She had learned to drive.
She had gone on trips.
She had fixed up the house.
She had helped people and herself.
And now
she was going out
with a new man.

Mollie asked,
"Is this really me?"

"Sure, it's you,"
said Rita.
"Your life
is far from over.
You have to live it."

Mollie was happy
about all the things
she had done.
She had never thought
she could do
such things.
But she had.
She had done them

on her own,
and she had
done them well.

"It *is* my life,"
said Mollie.
She had a happy look
on her face.
"I *do* have to live it.
And you know what, Rita?
I feel good about it.
I feel really good."

Mollie walked back
toward her house.
The sun was going down.
Soon it would come up again.

Thinking It Over

1. Do you think
it's important
to know how
to live alone?
Why or why not?

2. What have you done
in the last year
to grow as a person?

3. What could you do
in the next year
to grow as a person?

4. What do the last few lines
of the book
mean to you?